Lily Brown's Paintings

Lily Brown's Paintings

BY ANGELA JOHNSON   PAINTINGS BY E. B. LEWIS

ORCHARD BOOKS · NEW YORK
AN IMPRINT OF SCHOLASTIC INC.

For Henry Halem and all that he sees.
—ANGELA JOHNSON

All children are artists. The problem is how to remain an
artist once he grows up. — PABLO PICASSO
—E.B. LEWIS

ISBN-13: 978-0-545-09952-3
ISBN-10: 0-545-09952-8

Text copyright © 2007 by Angela Johnson. Illustrations copyright © 2007 by E. B. Lewis.
All rights reserved. Published by Scholastic Inc. SCHOLASTIC, ORCHARD BOOKS, and associated logos are trademarks and/or registered trademarks of Scholastic Inc.

12 11 10 9 8 7 6 5 4 3 2 1   8 9 10 11 12 13/ 0

Printed in the U.S.A.   08

This edition first printing, September 2008

The art was created using watercolors.

The text type was set in 19-point Dundee Bold.

Book design by Kristina Albertson

Note From E. B. Lewis

As a child, my father would take me to work at the Philadelphia Museum of Art. Surrounded by the images of some of my favorite artists, Van Gogh, Gauguin, Matisse, and Klee, I felt inspired. The museum was the playground where my artistic imagination first soared. I imagine that Lily Brown is similarly influenced by an early childhood exposure to the arts.

Perhaps these early experiences help fuel her vivid imagination and fascination with painting, much like my early exposure to the Masters did for me. In Lily Brown's Paintings *I find myself paying homage to the artists and having fun with the art I love. A couple of my favorite scenes include Van Gogh's bedroom scene where Lily dances around freely, and the scene where Lily is captivated by a story told by the storyteller on Gauguin's beach.*

Lily Brown loves her mama, daddy, and baby brother and the world they live in.

Sometimes she spins around her room thinking about their world. And it's wondrous.

But when Lily Brown paints,
her world starts to change.

The sunlight turns to stars, and Lily begins flying around them. All the universe is one big colorful splash.

The stars circle the planets in Lily Brown's paintings. . . .

And sometimes they come down to earth to hang around sidewalk cafés and shine when the sun goes down.

When Lily Brown paints,
the trees that she walks
past on her way to school
wear hats and drink tea
on cool days with other trees
and shrubbery.

They know Lily
and bow to her.

When Lily Brown paints fruit
at the corner market,
it is striped and polka-dotted.
It speaks to people,
then laughs out loud.

When people put the
fruit in bags to take home,
the apples sing all the way there.

In Lily Brown's paintings
the path to the park becomes
a wild-animal living room
with antelopes lounging and
alligators on the phone.

Lily always remembers
to draw them a treat.

In Lily Brown's paintings
softly blowing rose-colored winds
bring voices from across the ocean
to tell stories that she has never heard.

Then she listens . . .
and paints with blues and orange
to let the wind know
she has heard them.

Sometimes Lily herself
walks around in her paintings
or sails away through fields of red corn
and purple-painted skyscrapers.

In Lily Brown's paintings
the colors of people,
places, and things
change with her heart.

People walk upside down,
and the buildings on streets dance
with airplanes flying above.
And it's another world.

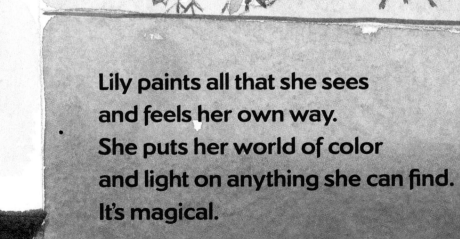

Lily paints all that she sees
and feels her own way.
She puts her world of color
and light on anything she can find.
It's magical.

But,
at the end of the day when Lily Brown
is about to put her paints away,
she remembers her mama's smile,
her daddy's eyes,
and the way her baby brother
holds her hand before he goes to sleep.

Baby Mac

Me

It's their world again,
and it's wondrous.